NAKED THOUGHTS

EVERYTHING I NEVER SAID OUT LOUD

KAMWANG

Made with ♥ on the Notion Press Platform
www.notionpress.com

To the ones who saw the surface but never stayed long enough to understand the depth. To the versions of me I've outgrown, and the ones I'm still learning to forgive. To the nights I couldn't sleep because my thoughts were louder than the world outside. To the days I smiled, and no one noticed it was breaking me. To the silence that followed every "I'm fine." To the dreams I buried under responsibility, and the love I gave away without a receipt. To everyone who ever made me feel like I was too much—or not enough. You made me write. And to you—yes, you. The one holding this book. May you find a piece of yourself in these pages, and realize you were never alone in the dark.

**'Sometimes I wonder if I'm living,
or just surviving in a life I didn't ask for—
breathing in moments that feel more like memories
of someone I used to be.'**

Contents

Contents

Foreword

I never meant to write a book.

I just had too many thoughts that refused to be silenced.

Words became my way of bleeding without making a mess.

And over time, those quiet breakdowns—scribbled in late-night notes, unsent texts, and the corners of my mind—turned into poems.

This collection isn't polished to impress.

It's not always pretty.

But it's real.

It's about the ache of failing when everyone expects you to rise. It's about heartbreak that doesn't always come from love, but from people, from life, from yourself.

It's about staring at your ceiling wondering what went wrong—when nothing did, and everything did, all at once.

You'll find pieces here that sound like you. Or someone you used to be. Or someone you're scared of becoming.

Some of these poems are loud. Others barely whisper.

But every one of them is honest.

And sometimes, that's all we have.

So, this is for the ones who overthink, who feel too much, who break quietly.

This is for the ones who want to be heard, even if it's just on paper.

This is for you.

Thank you for reading.

Thank you for staying.

- The writer who never meant to write.

Preface

This book is a mirror I never wanted to hold.

Each poem is a piece of me I tried to hide, then scribbled down just to breathe.

I didn't write these words to be understood—I wrote them to understand myself.

Over the years, I changed. Drastically.

From being the kid who was "gifted" to someone who fumbles through failure, doubt, heartbreak, and identity.

The journey wasn't linear. Some days I rose. Most days I fell.

But every moment carved out a truth I could no longer keep in silence.

These poems are not fiction. They are fragments—of moments, of mental spirals, of late-night grief and quiet hope.

Some are about love. Some are about loss. Many are about that strange middle ground where you feel everything and nothing all at once.

I've learned that people will love the version of you that never asks too much.

But this book? It asks everything.

It asks to be seen, in all its messiness and vulnerability.

And if you see yourself in these pages—then maybe you weren't alone either.

Thank you for being here.

Even if you don't stay long.

Acknowledgements

This isn't the part where I thank a long list of people.

Because truthfully, there wasn't one.

No team. No hand holding. No savior.

Just me—and the weight I carried alone.

So this, I dedicate to the sleepless nights.

To the spiral thoughts that wouldn't stop.

To the moments I thought I'd break, and still somehow didn't.

To the ache of being unseen, and the strength it took to keep going anyway.

I owe this to every version of me who felt too much and said nothing.

To the pain that sculpted me, to the silence that raised me.

To the breakdowns that taught me how to write.

To the vulnerability that cracked me open enough to bleed words on paper.

Thank you to the struggle.

To the sadness, the loneliness, the rage, the numbness—

The emotions that felt like enemies but ended up being the only ones who stayed.

If you're reading this, maybe you've met them too.

And maybe, just maybe, you'll find something here that understands you better than people ever could.

Prologue

I'm not a poet—not in the polished, literary sense of the word.

These poems weren't written to impress anyone. They don't follow form. They don't always rhyme. Some don't even have structure. And maybe that's the point.

I never really believed that poetry needed to wear a suit and tie. I don't think it has to be dressed up in metaphors or polished until it shines. I believe a poem is any thought that dares to bleed on paper. Any feeling too heavy to carry in silence. Any truth that you whisper to yourself at 3 a.m. when the world is quiet, and you're not pretending anymore.

These are those whispers.

Messy, unedited, naive. Sometimes they make sense. Sometimes they don't. But they're honest. That's all I can promise you—these poems are real. Written in the middle of breakdowns, or long after the pain had settled like dust in my bones.

I'm still learning. I'm a rookie. An amateur. But I'd rather be an honest rookie than a hollow expert.

This collection is a mirror of me—raw, unsure, scarred, but still trying. If you find something here that stirs something in you, then maybe that's poetry too.

Let's not chase perfection. Let's just feel.

1. Life

The way of the sea
Belongs to the moon...
The way of the moon
Belongs to the sky...
And even if jealous stars
Break and shatter
across the Milky Way,
I will still find heaven within myself.....

2. Coffee

Give me a cup, maybe two,
or I swear, I'll kill you.
I like it hot, not the least bit chilled,
Just one spoon of sugar, perfectly filled.
A splash of cream, smooth as a dream,
Gets me smiling, or so it would seem.
So brew it quick and fill my cup,
Because this is not a butter knife
Don't make me cut you up..

3. I'M TIRED

Afraid to close my eyes at night,
Afraid of losing the little light.
The dark feels heavy, it pulls me in,
A quiet battle I'll never win.
My eyes are red, my body's weak,
But peace is something I can't seek.
Her face appears, I see it clear,
A twisted smile that feeds my fear.
I try to fight, I try to run,
But every night, I'm coming undone.
My mind's a mess, it tears apart,
And breaks the pieces of my heart.
I'm tired of this, I'm tired of pain,
I'm tired of fighting in my brain.
If I give in, will I be free—
Or will the dark take all of me?

4. The Search

The search is on
But I can't find it
My brain is gone
Yet I don't mind it
I look down low
And gaze up high
Even check the fridge
Though I don't know why
Where did it go?
I sadly wonder
But in my head
There's only thunder
A banging crash
A horrid sound
It wraps around me
Drags me down

Please help me out
Can't take the strain
Search here and there
For my lost brain.

5. The True Beauty of You

6. Little Flower

It started like any normal day.
I noticed a little flower out the window.
Nevertheless, I leaned in and said,
"Hi," to which it replied, "Hello."
The conversation went on,
Every morning, I'd bring
A cup of coffee and cigarettes from my room
To sip and smoke while conversing.
It didn't take long for me to find comfort,
For this flower gave every thought
Of love, of any sort,
I could exchange for it, back and forth.
But then I realized how far it is from my grasp.
I am by the window, and it's floating like the stars.
It's like a wish that could never come true,
Dreaming and hoping that I'd be with you, little flower.

7. All on Me

Sunrise creepin' through the blinds,

I'm up again before it's time.

Coffee's brewing, bills are due,

Ain't nobody movin'—but I do.

Hold the weight like I don't mind,

Keep it movin', keep it right.

You don't notice, but it's true—

The car, the house, the midnight cries,

The love, the loss, the sacrifice.

I don't ask, I don't plead,

But it's all on me.

Tires low, I fill the tank,

pick you up, don't hear no thanks.

Smilin' soft, but deep inside,

I wonder when I'll feel alive.

Hold the weight like I don't mind,

Keep it movin', keep it right.

You don't notice, but it's true—

Everything still runs 'cause I do.

It's all on me, yeahhh.

The car, the house, the midnight cries,

The love, the loss, the sacrifice.

NAKED THOUGHTS

I don't ask, I don't plead,
But it's all on me.

8. Rise From My Fall

Will you see my passion?
I plead on bended knee—
marry me,
become one with the fantasy.
Dreams of wanton desire
turn into fire.
Lay upon silk sheets,
and when our eyes meet,
we see the stars and kiss,
sharing the bliss.
I love you so much, baby—
please love me back.
For the love that you can give
creates the love that I lack.
I show you all of me,
and give you my all.
Stay with me longer,
so that I may rise
from my fall.

9. Deepest Fear

If you were to ask me my deepest fear,
I'd probably say something like spiders or the ocean.
People don't seem to look at you weirdly when you say that.
But if I were being truthful,
I'd tell you that my deepest fear
Is feeling the way I do-forever.
What if I always wake up
And am forever haunted
By what I see when I take off my clothes?
What if I never stop waking up each morning
Feeling like everything I do is pointless?
What if I end up lonely,
Miserable,
And alone?
But I don't think that's exactly what people
Really care to hear when they ask you
What your deepest fear is.
It's too real for them.
Too deep.
They probably wouldn't even know what to say.
So for now,

KAMWANG

I guess I'll just have to pretend
That my deepest fears are something
That's easy for others to swallow.

10. A Failure

I failed again—
and suddenly, I'm not who I used to be.
Once the gifted kid, now just a name
on a paper marked in red ink and shame.
They said I was smart,
said I'd go far.
But now I just stare
at my ceiling in the dark.
I tried—I really did.
But trying doesn't matter
when all they want is perfect.
And all I have are pieces.
No one checks in.
No one sees the shift—
from praise to pressure,
from hope to drift.
My strength has thinned,
my smile feels fake,
my mind is loud,
but my future feels blank.
Why me?

KAMWANG

Or maybe...
why still me?

11. The Masked Poet

A masked poet stumbles into night,
not even drinking
could drown his plight.
He doesn't want to show
his face,
due to the misery
that can't be replaced.
He wrote a poem
about a woman he loves,
for the king's henchmen
knew who she was.
He couldn't have her,
but though he tried,
the moment he did,
his notoriety had died.
Casted out of the realm,
the poet dreamed of her—
the times he spent lost,
his mind was such a blur.
This is the poem he had written,
so please stick around,
I'm sure you'll be smitten.

by a love so deep, it never drowned.

12. A Reason To Be

All writers are different.
I do it for sadness.
I do it for loss.
I do it for grief.
I do it to live.
When I pick up a pen,
it's because I'm done.
I've let this world run me into the ground,
I've slipped and fallen down—
into a hole I can't escape.
This endless agony
seems to be my fate.
With so much to learn
and so much to do,
so much to see,
but still, I can't find a reason—
a reason to be.

13. Does God Get Sad?

God knows everything
Every thought and action
He's never surprised
That must be a sad existence
Never feeling the euphoria
Of an unexpected blessing
I reckon it's lonely on the throne
Already knowing every outcome
Humans are a messed-up kind
But at least we can still be shocked
Like the day you said you loved me
And for once, I wished He didn't know.

14. A Poet Knows

To be a poet
is a lonely thing.
must have been hurt
by many of things.
You must have failed
a lot in your life,
to know your emotions,
to feel when you write.
You cannot just say
pretty words that rhyme.
It's not about rhythm,
it's not about time.
It's only about
the feelings you see,
for poetry is you,
and poetry is me.
But one thing is certain,
one thing you must know—
if you're a true poet,
your emotions will flow.
Your ink spills like tears
on a paper of fears.

Your eyes see wonder,
yet carry the years.
Hold these truths
from the very start—
because being a poet
flows from the heart.

15. The Light You Left In Me

Every path in life has led me to you.
Even if I take a road to forget,
it will only turn me back to you.
We found each other not by choice,
not by chance, nor by mistake.
We never drained; we only grew.
I watered you, and you did too.
So let's keep growing, side by side.
Even if a thousand hearts adore you,
their love would be a single drop
against the ocean I hold for you.
And know this—my door is always open.
You may enter, you may leave,
without a word, without a plea.
Whatever choice your heart may make,
I will accept it, wholeheartedly.
But if one day the world feels cold,
and the weight of life too much to hold,
turn around—you'll find me there,
waiting, always, with open arms.

16. Cold

I don't write poems
I'm not a poet
But here I am, trying to show it
With boring words, clumsy rhymes
Cliché phrases lost in time
Ha, who am I kidding?
I can't solve it so fitting
I know that for years, decades
I'll fight on as my courage fades
What my passion? What can I do?
What should I give? What must I lose?
Will I change my stubborn ways?
Or regret my past on my final days?
How can I leave a mark so small
In a world where I feel nothing at all?
Questions, questions, left unheard
Spiraling, spiraling, like a caged bird
I know I must move to find what's right
But I stay in my warmth, avoiding the fight
Yet am I truly at peace in this place?
Or is stillness a trap I'm scared to face?
The blanket of comfort shields me outside

But deep within, the cold won't subside
I have to shake off this bitter cold
So I hum a tune, let warmth take hold
For a moment, it feels okay
But when I peek beyond my stay
It's freezing—so freezing, sharp like a knife
So I shrink back in, clinging to life
Shaking from the newfound chill
Cold inside, uncertain still
Frustrated with myself, yet here I stay
Afraid to leave, afraid to stray.

17. My Sanity

I wonder if
I'm even sane
Is there a piece
left of my brain?
Or have I gone
too far to mend
Approaching now
my witless end?
One thing I know
about my mind—
I've outlasted most
of humankind.

18. Twenty

Twenty is more than a number, bigger than you think
Like having twenty errands or twenty thoughts to overthink
What if you wrote twenty poems, or even twenty-five
About one girl, like I did, who makes me feel alive
She's got twenty sparks in her soul, and a heart of gold
And I'll still love her in twenty years, until we're both old
She's got twenty things about her that I admire
And when I'm with her, I feel twenty times hotter than fire
There are twenty reasons why she's the one I adore
But now and always, I'll love her twenty times more.

19. Why?

They say life is one staircase,
And as I go up,
I see it is the same as at the bottom.
A cliff is the best image of that.
One step is all you need.
But the thing is,
Which way do you want to go?
Do want to go back into the dark,
Or do you want to find the spark
That makes it perfect?
Again and again, the same question is asked,
What to do now?
The answer is unknown,
Heart telling one, mind another.
Isn't that strange?
Why does it even happen?
Why the hell did I spend all that time?
Why, why?
Just stranded in one place,
Waiting for a text that won't come.
But why?It's always, why.
Hope just stays there to fulfill her job,

A job that just makes me keep asking,
WHY?

20. MY OWN WAY

I don't remember my first,
My first poem.
I don't think I even knew
What I was trying to do.
When I had that pen,
That pen in my hand,
It didn't take long to understand.
I felt my emotions rush the page.
No one ever taught me,
Taught me the ways.
No one gave me the key,
The keywords to say.
I write with my emotions,
I give the page my devotion.
I write to maybe,
Maybe inspire someone.
My words may not make
Make sense at all.
My words might,
Might make tears fall.
The point is this:
If you leave the page bare,

Your emotions could be anywhere,
Waiting for the shift.
The way I feel,
The way I am,
Helps me write.
It's not all black and white.
My poems
Don't follow rules.
My poems
Are still true.
Words-
That's all it is.
Words-
That's all it ever will be.
Emotions-
That's what makes a poem.
Emotions-
That's where we all relate.
I will always write,
Write in my own way.
I will always write,
Write until my last day.

21. Apathy

I don't know why people say,
That hate and love are opposites in a way.
But I don't buy it, not at all,
For that idea is bound to fall.
Love makes you feel all kinds of things,
Joy and sorrow, the pain it brings.
Jealousy, longing, regret so deep,
Yet hate is just another feeling we keep.
You may hate the one who caused you pain,
Or hate the walls that block your way.
But hate itself is born from love,
Not something that stands above.
If I must name love's true foe,
I'd think awhile and let it show.
It's not hate—it's something cold,
Apathy, where no hearts hold.

22. Broken

My words aren't coming
My pages stay blank
Is this all your doing?
Was this all your plan?
I came to you to confess my heart
But you spoke of him right from the start
"Oh," I said, "good for you"
What else could I even do?
My chest feels heavy, worse than before
I try to write, but my head is sore
It burns, it burns deep inside
It hurts so much, yet doesn't bleed outside
How cruel it is, this unseen pain
A wound so deep, yet not a stain

23. My Pathetic Self

I feel like I got new glasses,
And now I can see
What everyone else has seen
All along—me.
My heart is pounding in my chest,
Because I hate the new, same old me.
Is any of this real?
Was my happiness just fake?
Disappointed in myself again
For making the same mistake.
Here I am again,
Disappointed in my mentality.
Here I am again,
Afraid of this reality.
Here I am again,
Silent, sullen, and depressed-
On the verge of another breakdown,
Once again, I'm distressed.
I feel like the lights have switched on,
And everyone is staring.
Clearly, I'm not quite right,
But everyone has stopped caring.

Is any of this real?
Have I mentally crossed a line?
Disappointed in myself again—
"I'm sure that I'll be fine."
Here I am again,
Afraid of my capacity.
Here I am again,
Disappointed in my tenacity.
Here I am again,
Lonely, illogical, and bleak—
On the verge of screaming,
Yet not finding the words to speak.
I'm two breaths shy of normal,
And the panic's setting in.
Did all the self-care and therapy,
But it's all happening again.
Those thoughts scream in my head,
Like someone set an alarm.
I'm scrubbing my frontal lobe
Of self-hate and self-harm.
I feel like my blindfold has been removed,
And I've been alone this whole time.
So many felonies and misdemeanors—
And I'm the only one charged with the crime.
Is any of this real?
More importantly, is it permanent?
Disappointed in myself again—

A disappointment I can't prevent.
Here I am again,
Disappointed in my weakness.
Here I am again,
Afraid of my bleakness.
Here I am again,
Reliving, rewinding, and consumed.
Used to believe that I'd be fine-
And now I can't help but feel I'm doomed.

24. Dumb

Jaw clenched
Eyes wide
Pupils dilated
Sleepless nights
Uncomfortable days
To get so high
Only to feel so low
It has never made sense to me-
Yet I continue to bring myself
Right back to this feeling.
So overwhelmed and sensitive,
But completely emotionless at the same time.
Self-hatred and disgust,
Yet also self-aware and content.
Crying one minute,
Numb the next-
Always an absolute train wreck.
All aboard the hot mess express.
Why do I do this to myself?

25. Hierarchy

You can't tell a fish to climb a tree,
Nor can you ask a bird to swim in the sea.
A fish can hold its breath forever,
But a bird is free to fly wherever.
Just because the fish swims deep
Doesn't mean the bird's worth is cheap.
Humans see them as different beings,
Yet judge each other by the same things.
Just because we share the same features
Doesn't mean we're the same kind of creatures.
If I fail my math exam,
It feels like my future is damned.
That's how the system in this world works—
Everyone must excel, no room for quirks.
But a bird doesn't swim to survive,
And a fish doesn't fly to stay alive.
So why does grade decide our fate?
Why must failure equate hate?
Even if I'm not as smart as you,
I'm still worth the same—and that's true.

Afterword

If you've made it this far, thank you—for reading, for staying, for listening. These words were not meant to be polished diamonds. They are rough stones picked from the riverbed of my thoughts—wet, heavy, unshaped. But they are mine.

This book was never about perfect poetry. It was about surviving. About bleeding safely onto pages. About making sense of things I couldn't explain out loud. These poems were written in silence, in tears, in sleepless nights and empty mornings. They're the pieces of someone who is still learning how to exist.

If even one line made you feel seen, then this wasn't in vain. If none did, then maybe it was just meant to be heard, not understood.

And maybe that's okay too.

"We don't write to be remembered. We write because we couldn't forget."

– kamwang